Skittles Riddles

Math

BITE SIZE CANDIES

Barbara Barbieri McGrath
Illustrated by Roger Glass

Charlesbridge

The author would like to thank the following "sweet" people for their help: Will M., Paul L., Mary Ann and Nina, Harold, and Yo. A special thank-you goes to Marilyn Shepard and the staff at Charlotte Dunning Elementary School in Framingham, Massachusetts.

riddle (rĭd'l) *n. A question or statement requiring thought to answer or understand; a conundrum*

* *definition from* The American Heritage Dictionary of the English Language, *third edition, Houghton Mifflin Company, 1996.*

Text copyright © 2000 by Barbara Barbieri McGrath
Illustrations copyright © 2000 by Roger Glass
All rights reserved, including the right of reproduction in whole or in part in any form.

Published by Charlesbridge Publishing
85 Main Street, Watertown, MA 02472
(617) 926-0329
www.charlesbridge.com

Library of Congress Cataloging-in-Publication Data
McGrath, Barbara Barbieri, 1954–
    Skittles® bite size candies riddles math/Barbara Barbieri McGrath; illustrated by Roger Glass.
        p. cm.
    ISBN 1-57091-412-5 (reinforced for library use)
    ISBN 1-57091-413-3 (softcover)
    1. Mathematics—Study and teaching (Elementary)
[1. Mathematics.] I. Glass, Roger, ill. II. Title.
QA135.5.M4547   2001
372.7'044—dc21   00-038372

Printed in South Korea
(hc) 10 9 8 7 6 5 4 3 2 1
(sc) 10 9 8 7 6 5 4 3 2 1

Illustrations in this book done in Adobe Photoshop and Adobe Illustrator
Display type and text type set in Adobe Stone Sans and Serif
Printed and bound by Sung In Printing, Inc., South Korea
Production supervision by Brian G. Walker
Designed by Roger Glass
Computer graphics by Blue Moon Studio, Inc.

With love to Kiley B.
— B.B.M.

With love to Kel
— R.G.

Here's the first riddle. Now get ready—let's go!
What has five bright colors and tastes like a rainbow?

There are five fruity colors in a bag of SKITTLES® Original Bite Size Candies. What's your favorite flavor?
Red is strawberry, yellow is lemon, green is lime, purple is grape, and orange is . . . well, orange.

SKITTLES® are bite-sized, and SKITTLES® are fun.
Pour them. Sort them. Math magic has begun!

SKITTLES® Riddle:
Why are SKITTLES® Original
Bite Size Candies
always happy?

A: Because they're never blue!

Choose one color to count. Now let's compare.
Is yours greater or less than the other colors there?

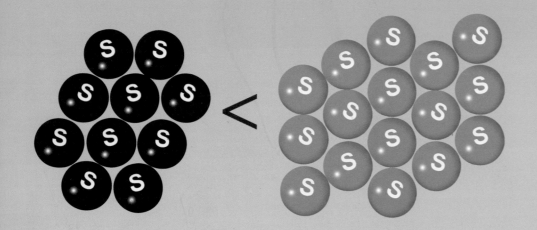

When comparing the quantities of objects, the symbol < means "less than," and the symbol > means "greater than."

Number sentences are easy, if you know how to count.
The purple plus orange equals what total amount?

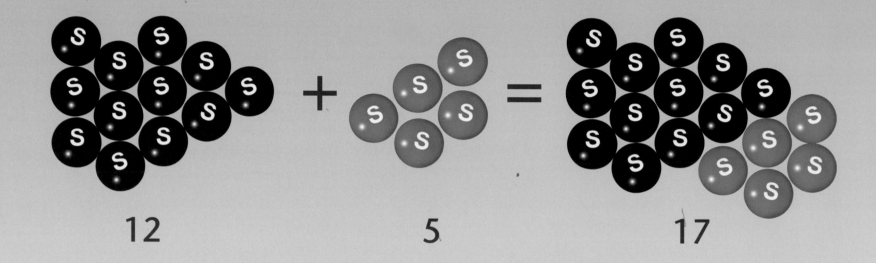

12   5   17

Now make three more number
sentences beginning with purple
and adding another color.
Can you solve these math mysteries?

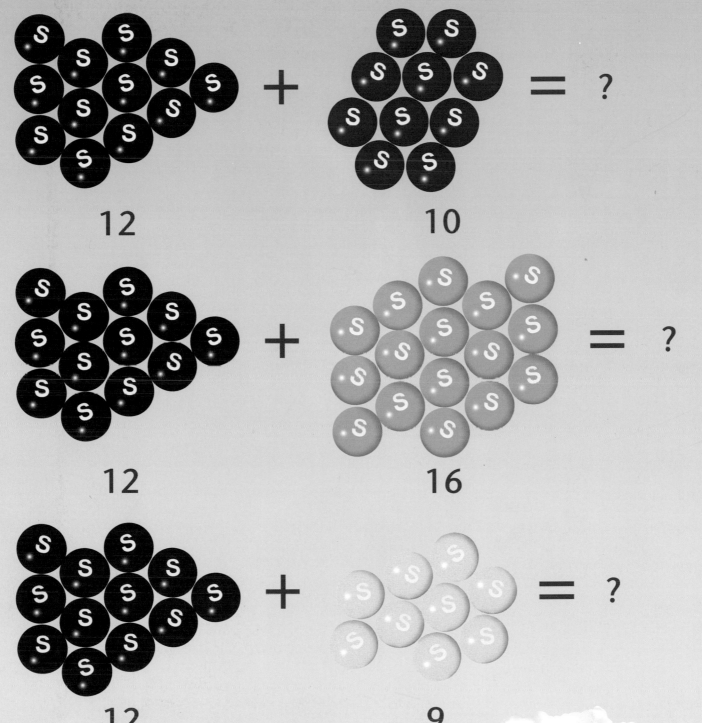

12 + 10 = ?

12 + 16 = ?

12 + 9 = ?

Now use subtraction to take nine from sixteen.
Notice the symbol for subtraction in between.

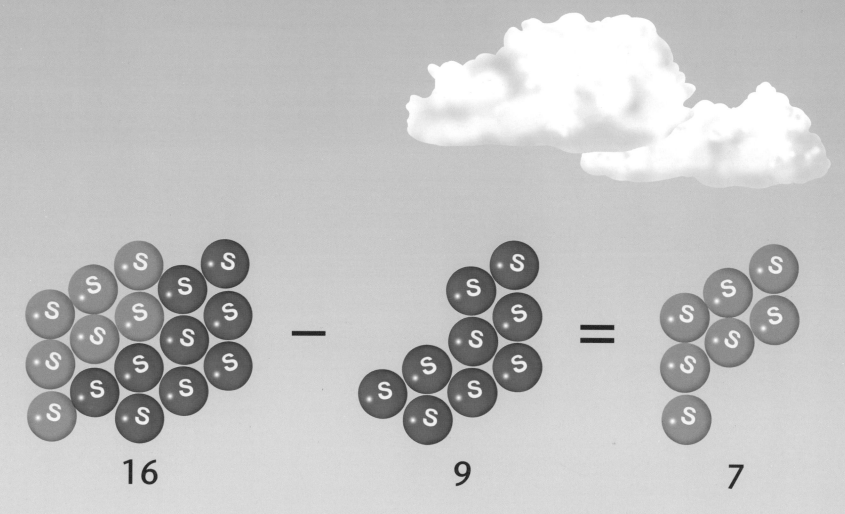

16   9   7

How many subtraction sentences can you make?
Subtract the smaller number from the larger number.

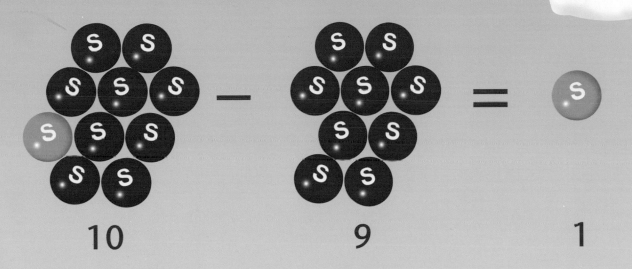

10   9   1

SKITTLES® Riddle:

Did you know math problems could be riddles?
Try this one: Sixteen SKITTLES® Candies minus how many equals four?

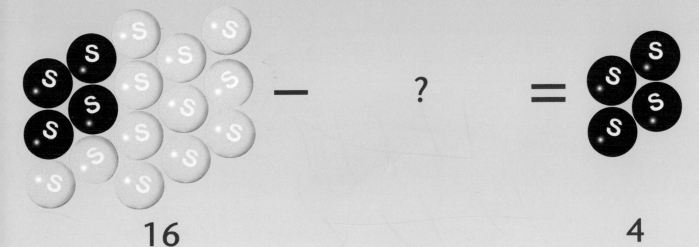

16   ?   4

If you want to get tricky,
use a number line to subtract
the larger number from the
smaller number. Confused?
Keep reading. . . .

A: Sixteen minus twelve makes four.

Negative numbers are those less than zero.
Use the number line here to become a math hero!

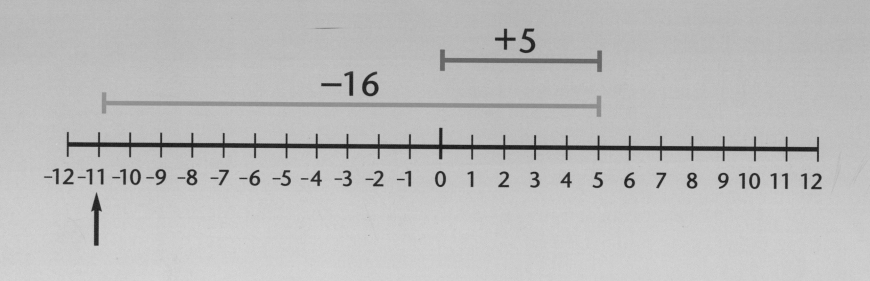

$$5 - 16 = -11$$

On a number line, the positive numbers (numbers greater than zero) are to the right of zero, and the negative numbers (numbers less than zero) are to the left of zero.

SKITTLES® Riddle:
What do infinity and a
rainbow have in common?

A: Both have no end! Can you imagine what
an infinite amount of SKITTLES® Candies
would look like?

To the land of fractions let us proceed.
You'll find these pie graphs helpful indeed.

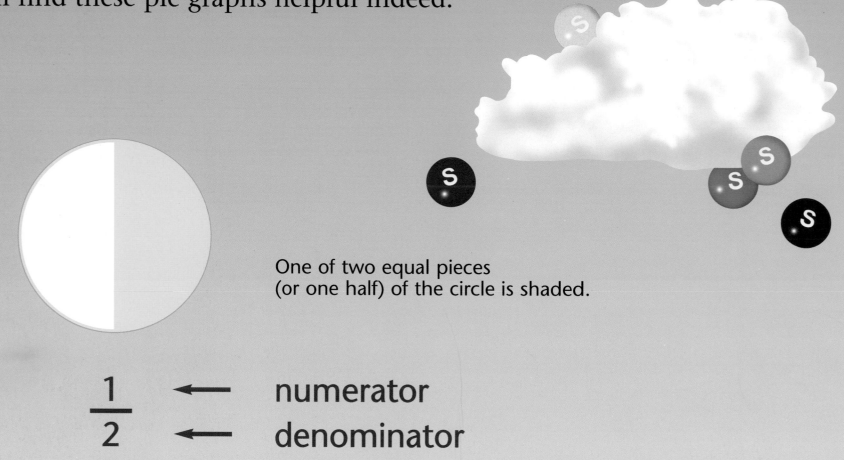

One of two equal pieces
(or one half) of the circle is shaded.

$$\frac{1}{2}$$

1 ← numerator

2 ← denominator

A fraction is a number that expresses part of a whole or a set. SKITTLES® Candies can help make colorful fractions! When writing fractions, the number on top is called the numerator, and the number under it is called the denominator. Here's an easy way to remember which is which: denominator begins with the letter *d*, and *d* = down.

These are pie graphs. It's helpful to think of fractions as part of a circle. These three pie graphs show one fourth, one third, and three fourths.

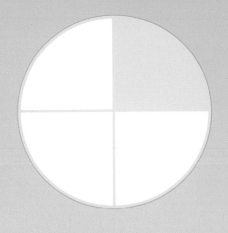

$$\frac{1}{4}$$

$$\frac{\text{one piece}}{\text{four total pieces}}$$

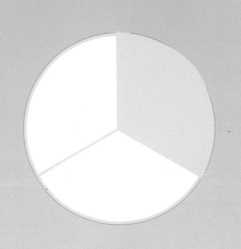

$$\frac{1}{3}$$

$$\frac{\text{one piece}}{\text{three total pieces}}$$

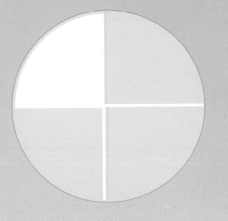

$$\frac{3}{4}$$

$$\frac{\text{three pieces}}{\text{four total pieces}}$$

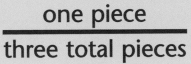

A group of five SKITTLES® is colorful and sweet. Each piece is one fifth, a fruity fraction treat.

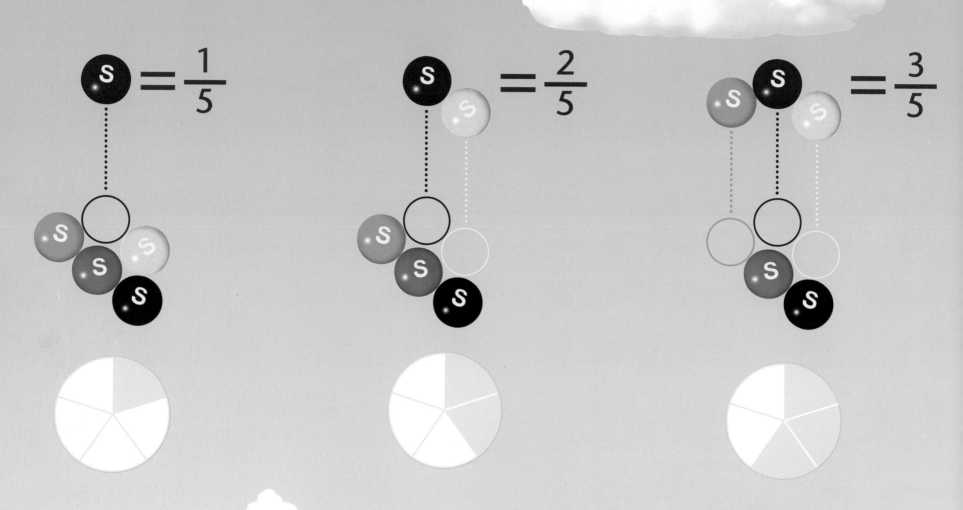

As you know, there are five colors in a bag of SKITTLES® Candies. If you have one of each color in your hand and you give one to a friend, then you have shared one fifth of the SKITTLES® Candies you were holding.

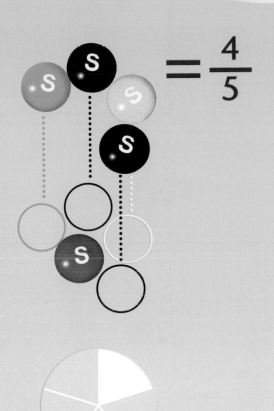 $= \dfrac{4}{5}$

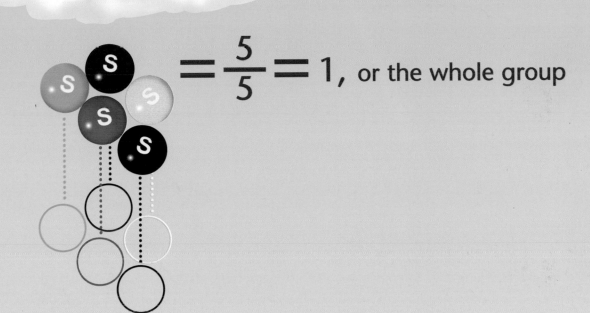 $= \dfrac{5}{5} = 1$, or the whole group

Which fraction is bigger? It sure can be confusing.
You need to look at the actual amount you are using.

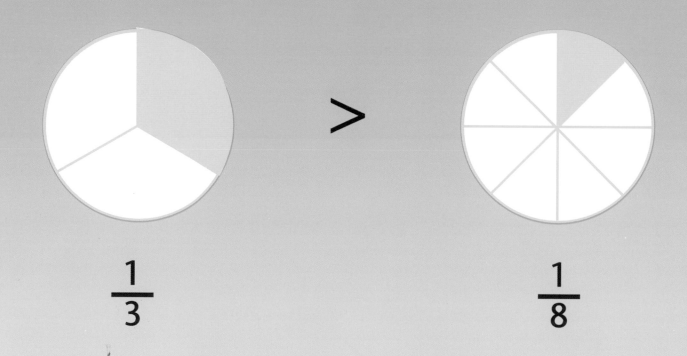

$$\frac{1}{3} \quad > \quad \frac{1}{8}$$

You might think that the fraction one eighth is bigger than one third. After all, eight is greater than three. But this is how those two fractions actually look. As you can see, one third is definitely larger than one eighth.

SKITTLES® Riddle:
Which fraction is larger, one fifth or one twentieth?

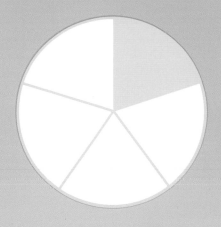

$$\frac{1}{5}$$

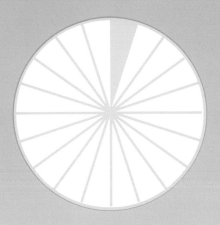

$$\frac{1}{20}$$

A: One fifth.

Sort out five of four colors, so now there are twenty.
To learn more about fractions, this will be plenty.

= 20 candies

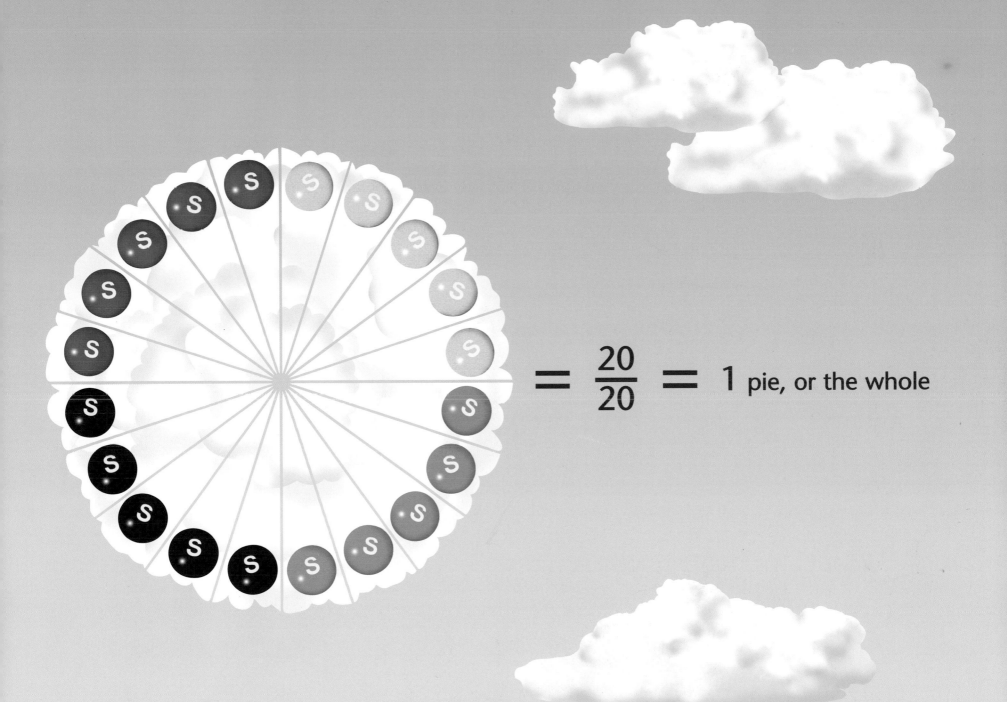

$$= \frac{20}{20} = 1 \text{ pie, or the whole}$$

Five twentieths represents each color you see.
One fourth is its equal, if you look carefully.

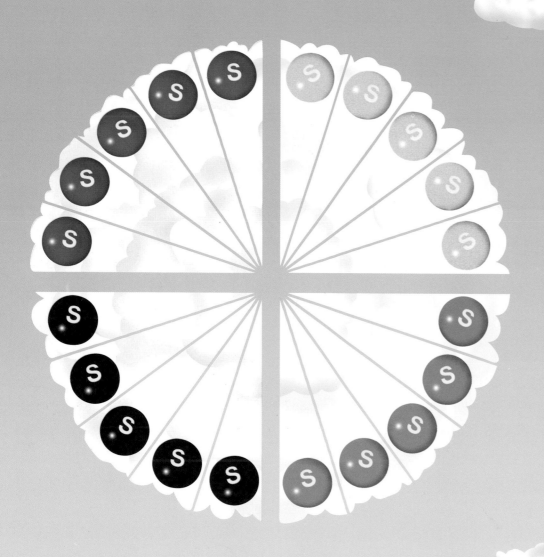

Each color is $\dfrac{1}{4}$ of the whole pie.

To reduce fractions to their lowest terms, or simplest forms, you must figure out by what number both the numerator and denominator can be divided. What's that number for this fraction?

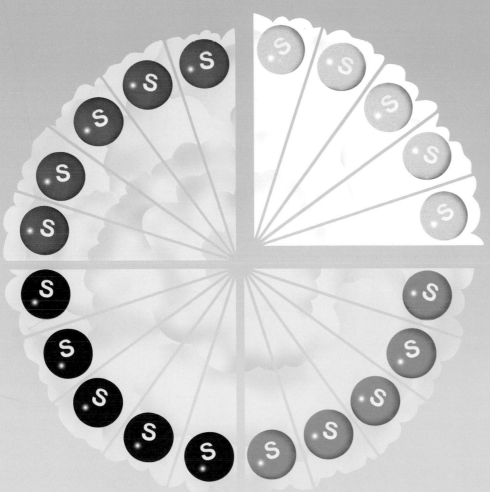

$$= \frac{5}{20} \div \frac{5}{5} = \frac{1}{4}$$

The numerator and denominator can both be divided by five:
$5 \div 5 = 1$, and $20 \div 5 = 4$.

SKITTLES® Riddle:
What do SKITTLES® Candies and fractions have in common?

A: It's fun to reduce them!

Fractions can be tricky; they have more than one name.
Ten twentieths, five tenths, and one half all mean the same.

$$\frac{10}{20}$$

$$\frac{5}{10}$$

$$\frac{1}{2}$$

$\frac{10}{20}$ reduces to $\frac{5}{10}$:

$\frac{5}{10}$ reduces to $\frac{1}{2}$:

So, $\frac{10}{20} = \frac{5}{10} = \frac{1}{2}$

$$\frac{10}{20} \div \frac{2}{2} = \frac{5}{10}$$

$$\frac{5}{10} \div \frac{5}{5} = \frac{1}{2}$$

For an extra challenge, let's add two fractions together. To do this, the denominator of each fraction must be the same, or common. One fourth plus one fourth equals two fourths! Which reduces to one half! Wasn't that easy?

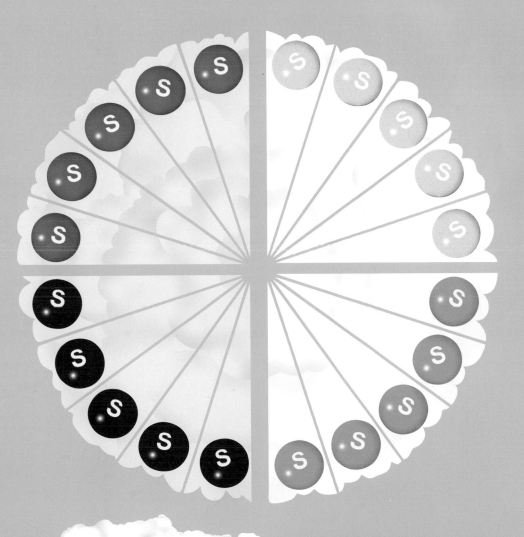

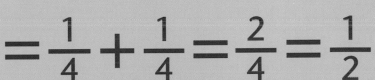

$$= \frac{1}{4} + \frac{1}{4} = \frac{2}{4} = \frac{1}{2}$$

SKITTLES® Riddle:
If you have three sixths of a pie and your friend has four eighths of a pie, who has more?

A: Neither! Both fractions reduce to one half.

In fraction form let's add yellow, red, and green.
Fifteen twentieths equals three fourths, as is clearly seen.

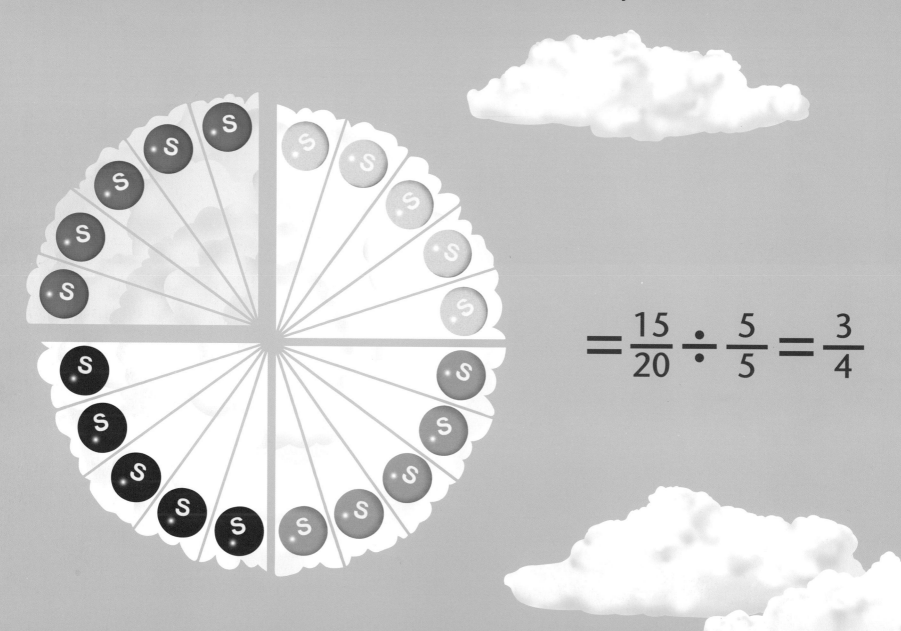

$$= \frac{15}{20} \div \frac{5}{5} = \frac{3}{4}$$

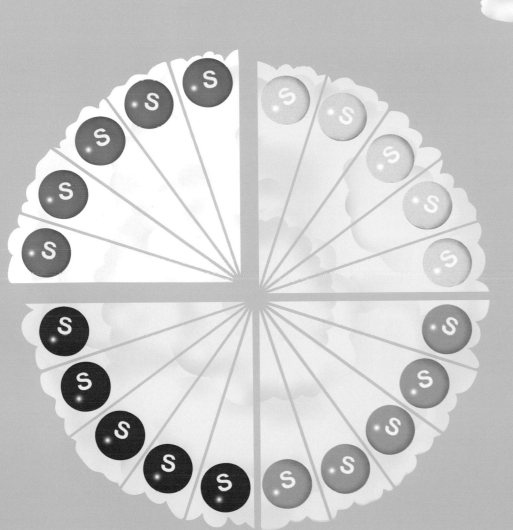

$$= \frac{4}{4} - \frac{3}{4} = \frac{1}{4}$$

If you remove three fourths of the pie, then there is only one quarter of the pie left. How would you say the fraction that would use the whole pie? Let's see. . . .

Reducing twenty twentieths to lowest terms is our goal.
The answer's one over one; this represents a whole.

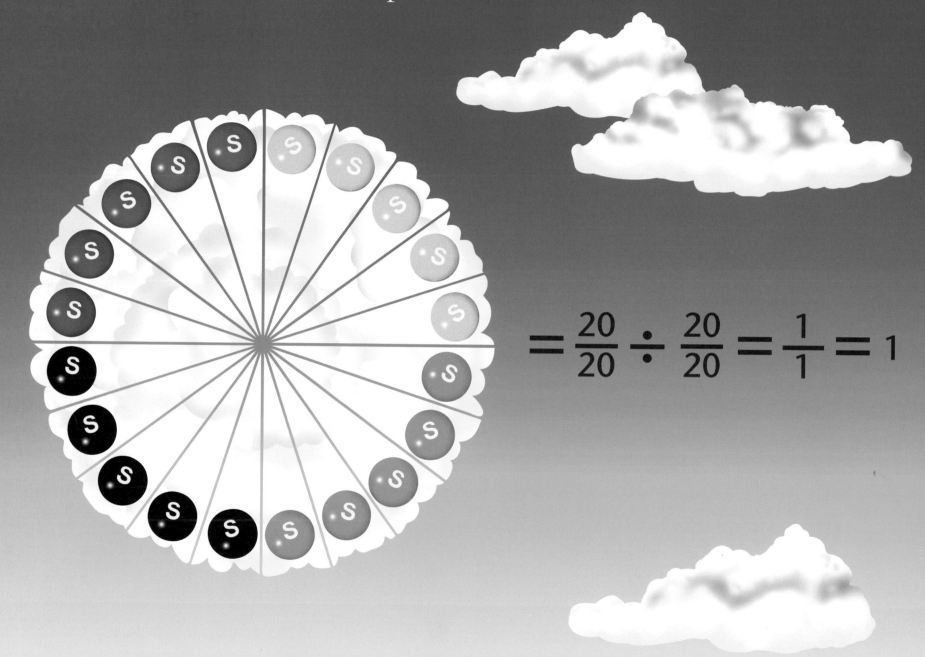

$$= \frac{20}{20} \div \frac{20}{20} = \frac{1}{1} = 1$$

Now we have used the whole pie.
Who knew fractions could be so delicious?

Make the SKITTLES® vanish! The math is all done.
Please make a wish as you eat the last one.

SKITTLES® Riddle:
What's the magic of SKITTLES® Bite Size Candies?

A: Making them disappear!

With the wonder of numbers and the flavor of SKITTLES®, use your imagination to create your own riddles!

Math Terms

common denominator: the number into which all the denominators in a group of fractions can be divided; when the denominators are common, or the same, calculations can be performed

denominator: the number either below or to the right of the line of a fraction; represents the total equal parts into which a whole has been divided; ex. $\frac{1}{2}$ or 1/**2**

equivalent fractions: fractions that represent the same amount; ex. 2/4 and 1/2

fraction: a part of a whole

infinity (∞): a never-ending, limitless quantity

fraction in lowest terms: a fraction reduced as far as possible by dividing the numerator and denominator by the same number

negative number: a number less than zero

number line: a line that shows numbers in order spaced uniformly above and below zero

number sentence: an expression of the relationship between numbers using mathematical symbols; ex. 3+5=8

numerator: the number either above or to the left of the line of a fraction; represents a certain number of parts of an equally divided whole; ex. $\frac{1}{2}$ or **1**/2

pie graph (also called *pie chart*): a circle divided into sections that represent parts of a whole

positive number: a number greater than zero

reduced fraction: a simplified fraction, achieved by dividing the numerator and denominator by the same number

whole fraction: a fraction that equals one, or all the parts of a whole; ex. 2/2, 4/4

Fraction Review

basic fractions

$$\frac{1}{2} \qquad \frac{1}{4} \qquad \frac{1}{3}$$

greater than and less than

$$\frac{1}{3} > \frac{1}{8} \qquad \frac{1}{8} < \frac{1}{3}$$

adding fractions

$$\frac{1}{4} + \frac{1}{4} = \frac{2}{4}$$

equivalent fractions

$$\frac{1}{2} = \frac{2}{4} = \frac{4}{8}$$

reducing fractions

$$\frac{5}{20} \div \frac{5}{5} = \frac{1}{4}$$

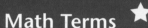